Grannie Knows Best

Grannie Knows Best

BIBLICAL BEDTIME STORIES

Aria L. Suber

Copyright © 2016 Aria L. Suber
All rights reserved.

ISBN: 0998111678
ISBN 13: 9780998111674

Grannie Knows Best: Biblical Bedtime Stories

Welcome, come on in! I'm Grannie. I look forward to sharing my stories with you, and I pray that you learn and grow from each story, it's never too early or too late to learn about God. Inside these pages, you'll see God loves all of us, and how we all have good and bad days. I try my best to point others in Gods direction.

Love,
Grannie

Stories

Who am I and why am I here?...1
Does God really love me?..3
Am I too young for GOD?..5
Where did Granddad go?...9
God, why do I wake up through the night?..........................12
Will God always help me?..15
Who is Satan?..18
How can I say thank you?..21
How do I share Jesus with my friends?..............................23
What should I do if I mess up, God?..................................26
What does it mean the Bible is alive?................................28
God, do you like to laugh?...30

Throughout these stories, you'll see "You can read" at the end of each story, this means you can read the bible scriptures listed to understand where Grannie gets her wisdom.

Who am I and why am I here?

JUNE IS IN THE FIFTH grade. On the bus ride home, a girl in her class said something that made June run to her grandmother, who sits on the porch and waits for the bus to arrive. June got off the bus and while running she was screaming, "Grannie! Grannie! This girl at school said I should've never been born and life has no need for me!"

Grannie looked and said, "All right, Ladybug, come on inside, and I'll tell you how I know that young girl was wrong." Since June has a summertime name, Grannie

calls her Ladybug. June loves her grannie and went there each day after school until her parents got off work. The two have a very special relationship, and when Grannie speaks, Ladybug listens.

As they sat in the kitchen for snacks, June said, "Grannie, how do you know she was wrong? She said life has no need for me."

"Remember when I said God made us all for a reason?" prompted Grannie.

June said, "Yes, Grannie, I remember."

"June, you and the same young girl that said those mean words have a purpose in life. Maybe you'll be a teacher, doctor, business owner, or even a beautiful grannie someday. But God has a plan for you, and you are wanted in this life," said Grannie. "You know what! God even knew he wanted Ladybug before he allowed a tree to grow." "You know when you tell your mom you'll save all the animals one day?" June replied with a big smile, "Yes, Grannie, and I will!"

"Well, Ladybug, that feeling you have is one of God's ways of letting you know that you're

meant to be in this life, and I believe you're going to work with animals someday. I'm sure you're going to do more great things.

June asked, "But why would she say that to me? I didn't say anything to her!"

"Well, Ladybug," Grannie explained, "people will say words that hurt or make you question yourself, but I want you to remember, no one can tell you that you

have no place in this life. Don't let words move the excitement that lives inside of you. Don't let them stop what you feel in your heart." June jumped up and hugged Grannie, and just then her parents arrived. June, "God willing, I'll be in the same place tomorrow, and I look forward to hearing all about your day."

You can read:
Ephesians 1:4-6 and Genesis 1:26-28 to learn more.

Does God really love me?

§

June is sleeping over at Grannie's house so she can attend her friend's birthday party who lives down the street from Grannie. As June was getting ready for bed, she asked Grannie if she could stay until she fell asleep. Grannie said, "I would love to, but only for a little while. When I was your age, my mom told me the same story every night." June was surprised. "You listened to the same story every night? I would've asked for a new one."

"Yes, you would have, my dear," Grannie said with a nod. "See, Ladybug, we didn't have all the fancy toys that your mom and dad can get you today, so bedtime stories meant the world to me. Today you have items to read you stories, like this in your hand, what is it called, a gPod?"

"No ma'am, Grannie," June replied as she laughed and told Grannie, "it's an iPod."

June and Grannie laughed together then Grannie said, "Click your button that records so you can have this story on the nights your old grannie isn't there to keep her Ladybug company." June showed Grannie the button and then got under the covers.

"Do you love me? I would ask the sky at night. One night my mother walked in and said, "Monk, who are you speaking to?" I'm talking to God, Mother. You said he loves us more than we know, and we can ask him anything." June asked with wonder, "What did your mom say?"

"Mother told me to get in the bed, covered me up; and sat by me like I'm sitting by you. Then she said, "You're right, Monk." June asked, "Monk? What's a Monk?"

"That's what my mother used to call me when I was little girl" and they laughed once more.

"My mother then said, 'Yes, he loves you, and we have reminders of that love. You can look at the sky, the land, eat His food, see His animals, and feel from the heart. God gave all these things to the people He loves, and He loves everybody all over the world."

"Yes, He loves you! God prepared a book to help you as you grow, and most importantly, He loves us all so much that He sent his only Son to cover us. Yes, Monk, God loves you, and don't you ever forget it," were the words my mother told me," Grannie explained.

Grannie looked, and June was fast asleep. Grannie said, "Ladybug, that's why I had to hear the same story every night, I too would fall asleep before my mother finished." Grannie clicked the button to stop recording, kissed June goodnight, and turned off the light.

You can read:
John 3:16, John 15:9-11, and 1 John 3:16 to learn more.

Am I too young for GOD?

GRANNIE IS PLANTING FLOWERS TODAY; she loves the break of spring when her annual flowers bloom. The kids and teens in the neighborhood know spring is the best time to make extra money. Jordan likes to help Grannie for more than money; Grannie helped him and his family, but she will never let his parents pay her back. Whenever he has the chance, he helps her in the yard.

"Hello, Jordan," Grannie said.

"Can I help you with anything today?" Jordan asked.

"Yes, you can help, but not in the yard. I know a young boy who needs assistance understanding that he can help God at any age," said Grannie.

Jordan said, "I remember when you had that talk with Marlon and me."

"I'm happy you do," said Grannie, "and I believe Jamal will benefit more if he hears from a cool young man versus a cool older lady."

Jordan laughed and said, "Grannie, I'll talk with him."

Sunday came, and after church, Grannie introduced the two. Jordan said, "I hear you think you're too young for God to use."

Jamal said, "Yes, all the people in the Bible are old!"

Jordan laughed and said, "Yes, some of them were, but some were younger than you. Did you know that kids ruled nations? Kings at eight years old? King Josiah was eight when he took over the Judah nation, and eighteen years later, he found out the way they were living was against God, and he called for everyone to live right in the sight of God. I love this king! He made a change that saved the people."

Jamal said, "No one ever said I could be a king!"

Jordan laughed again and said, "Calm down now. I didn't say that, but you can be used to help at age 12. I remember when I was your age."

"How old are you now?" Jamal asked.

"I'm 17," he replied, "and my brother Marlon, is 19 and in college."

"We thought there was no way God would use us," said Jordan.

Jamal then asked how God could use him. In a sad voice, he said, "I don't have anything to give."

Jordan said, "Marlon and I felt the same way. Our mom showed us in the Bible where a young boy named David won a great battle with a stone and the power of God. There was another young boy who had bread and fish. Jesus prayed over the meal and fed thousands of people with just a little boy's snack. I wish I could do that over my candy bars!" Jordan said the candy bar part to make Jamal laugh. "Oh yeah," said Jordan, "girls can even be used too."

Jamal was surprised. "They can?"

"Sure, God can use girls or boys. He used a girl named Miriam to save her baby brother, Moses, who later grew up and then God used him also, but he was older when God called on him.

"Marlon and I began helping people in the neighborhood. The neighbors started to pay us, and with that money, we were able to buy food for the homeless and food kitchens. We began to understand it's not about what we didn't have; it's about using what we did have. People need help in many ways. Some people just need you to listen to them, and when you start listening they try to talk your ears off!" The two boys laughed.

Jordan continued, "I can't believe I'm about to say this, but Grannie and my mom said some people just need a smile, and they were right. The point I'm making, kid, is this; there are many ways to be used, and you don't need money. Money just helps in others ways."

Just then Grannie came over and asked Jordan if everything was all right. He replied, "Yes, ma'am," in this cool voice. Jordan and Jamal shook hands before parting ways.

As Jordan walked home with Grannie, he told her, "I think God may use me to speak with people someday."

Grannie said, "Sweetie, he used you today."

You can read:
Exodus 2:1-10, John 6:9-15, 2 Kings 22, Matthew 19:14 and 1 Samuel 17 to learn more.

Where did Granddad go?

GRANNIE CURRENTLY HAS A HOUSE full of grandchildren. She has five. One lives in California, three live in New York City, and June lives in Kansas City, Kansas, along with Grannie. Grannie only sees the others twice a year but talks with them all the time. June is excited to see her cousins; Nathan, Tyler, Trey, and Brandi. The grandchildren always have such a good time together. Everyone has grown!

"This time next year, two of you will be in middle school and three in high school. Your granddad would have loved to see this," said Grannie. They all looked over and saw that Grannie had tears in her eyes.

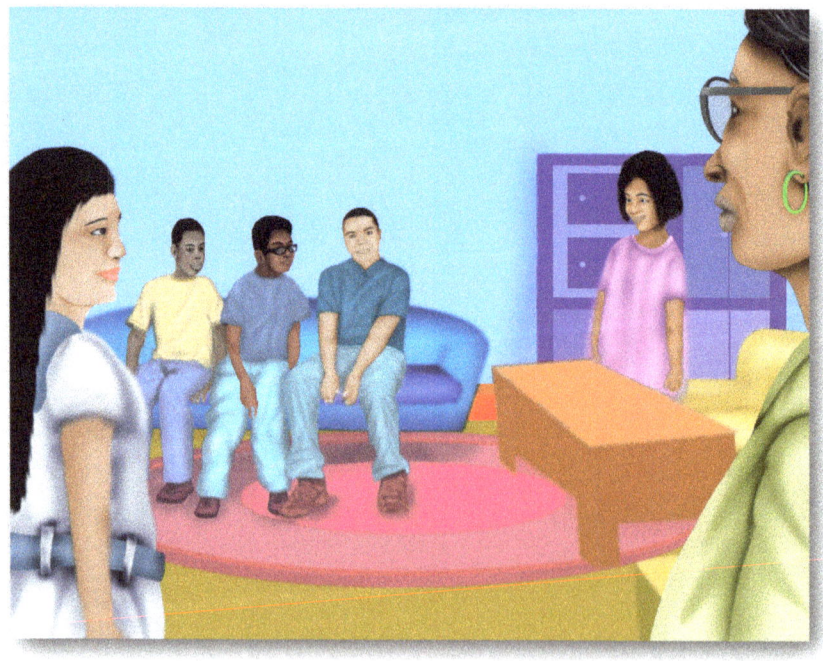

Trey said, "Grannie, it's okay, don't cry. You always say I have Granddad's directness. Nathan has Granddad's way to make everyone feel happy. Tyler has the mind to do things Granddad's way. June stays full of questions like him, and Brandi has his wisdom."

Grannie smiled and said, "You always know what to say, Trey."

Brandi then said, "Grannie, it always makes you feel better when you tell us where Granddad is." Grannie doesn't cry much, but whenever all the grandchildren get together, she thinks of the 40 years she and her husband shared together.

"Your granddad would always tell me. 'These grandchildren are God's way of saying I trust you with another life, but this life you can send back to their home.'"

Everyone laughed, and Brandi said again, "Where did Granddad go?"

Grannie smiled and said, "To a place where there are no tears and no pain. A place where he can be free and at peace. He went to be with Jesus."

Tyler asked, "Grannie, does everyone go with Jesus when they die?"

Grannie said, "Sweetie, in the Bible Paul said, "We are confident, yes, well pleased rather be absent from the body and to be present with the Lord." She paused for a moment and looked them all over then decided, "You're now old enough to get the rest of the story."

The grandchildren had heard the first part for years, but Grannie never told them some people would not go to this place of peace. "Some people make other choices, and Hell will be their home. But that's between them and God for the choices made on this earth. See, each day we awaken, we have a choice to live with Jesus, to be better, act better, speak better and treat others better. When we fall short—and we all do—we ask God to forgive us in Jesus name."

June inquired, "What happens to the people who don't ask for forgiveness and keep making the wrong choice?"

Grannie said, "The place they go will not have peace, Ladybug." She shook her head sadly. "Your grandad changed his life years ago and started living for Jesus. He wasn't perfect, but he was determined to please the Lord in all his ways. He knew he had to change some things, and I did too, for that matter. I know Granddad is in a place where we will all meet again and live together forever in peace, joy, and love."

After their talk, Grannie felt better and told the grandchildren, "You all head to the kitchen. I've got everyone's favorite toppings for ice cream sundaes."

Grannie Knows Best

    As they went towards the kitchen, Grannie stopped and looked at Granddad's picture and said, "After they eat their sundaes, I'm sending them downstairs to their parents." She laughed and walked toward the kitchen.

You can read:
2 Corinthians 5:6-10, Matthew 25:31-46 and Revelation 21:4 to learn more.

God, why do I wake up through the night?

THE GRANDCHILDREN ARE IN TOWN for one more night when Trey knocks on Grannie's door. Trey is 15, and he enjoys spending time with Grannie. "Grannie, are you asleep?"

"I'm up now, sweetie," Grannie said. "Come on in unless you're too big to jump in bed with Grannie." Trey said, "Grannie, I'll never be too big!" and he did a huge jump in the bed.

"What's going on, grandson? It's 3:00 a.m. Are you okay?"

Trey said, "Yes, ma'am, I just can't sleep lately. I turn on the TV, but I don't watch it. I get on my tablet, but I'd rather not do that, either. I just don't get it, Grannie. I like to sleep!"

Grannie then told him with a smile, "Sweetie, whenever anyone can't sleep like that, sometimes God himself could be waking you up."

Trey responded, "Waking me up for what?"

"Now, that I can't answer," said Grannie. "But your dad told me all about your interest in God here lately." Trey nodded. "I'll tell you what. I want you to read 1 Samuel chapter 1, verses 1 through 3. Once you understand it, call me and tell me why God is waking you up. I will say this, Trey, if God wants our attention, he can get it anytime!" Grannie said it with excitement. "But there's something special about those late hours and early mornings when your mind and body are still," Trey said he would read it, and they went back to sleep.

Some family friends stopped by, and Grannie made a big lunch before everyone drove to the airport. Two weeks later, as Grannie was waiting for June's school bus, she got a phone call.

Grannie: Hello?
Trey: Hi, Grannie, I understand it now!
Grannie: Do you? Tell me what you know, grandson. You sound excited!

Trey: Samuel was younger than I am. God called Samuel's name three times; maybe it's nothing, Grannie, but I wake up at 3:00 a.m. I think this is cool, the Maker of the world wants to spend time with me! Grannie, next time I wake up in the night I will pray, I'll even do like Samuel did and tell God I'm listening! I will also do more reading. I don't understand it all, but Dad said he would help me. He is going to help me understand how God speaks to us through his Holy Spirit. I'm willing to learn, what all of this means.

Grannie: Trey, you have made my day! And the more you read and are willing to learn, the more you will know. I think I need to start calling asking *you* questions now!

Trey: Grannie, I love you a whole lot, and I can't wait to see you again.

Grannie: I love you even more, and God willing, we'll see each other soon. You know you can call me anytime, for anything.

Trey: Yes, ma'am.

The call ended just as June's bus pulled up. Like always, June ran to meet Grannie. June asked, "Grannie, what has you so happy today?"

Grannie replied, "I just received a special call that touched my heart."

You can read:
John 15:26 and John 16:7, Matthew 10:20 and 1 Samuel 3:1-11 to learn more.

Will God always help me?

TODAY GRANNIE HEARD SOME WORDS that made her sad. As she was walking passed her gate, three teenagers walked by, and one said, "I don't think God will help someone like me." Now, Grannie didn't hear the whole conversation, but that statement didn't sit well with her. Grannie decided she would speak with the teenagers the next time she saw them in her neighborhood; she looked for several days, but they never showed up.

Two months later, Grannie was at a stop light six blocks from her house when she saw three teenagers walking towards a building that read "Youth Center." Grannie got that certain look on her face. She pulled right in front of the building, walked inside, and asked to speak with the person in charge. Grannie talked to the director of the building, who informed her that the teens attend a spiritual camp as part of the agreement to stay in the center.

Grannie figured they must have been talking about the camp the day she overheard them. Grannie invited the whole youth center to church service. She told Ms. Joyce, the director, I don't believe in forcing anyone to learn about God. That is a choice all people must make for themselves, but she would love to see them at service. Grannie headed to her car and again this certain look came over her face. She knew if they made a choice to come, many would learn something they would never forget.

Grannie spoke with the people of the church, and everyone was on board. They planned a special service for the youth center. A few Sundays passed, and no one from the youth center showed up. Grannie was a little sad, but she had realized a long time ago that everything happens in the Lord's time and not in Grannie's time.

One Sunday morning as Grannie was greeting members, she noticed a large van pull up in front of the church. She smiled and said, "Lord, your time is always the right time." Even Grannie thought they wouldn't come after so much time had passed. Grannie told Alayna to inform the other members the youth center had arrived; everyone knew the service that would take place.

The youth group was in charge of service; that's what made it special. A young man by the name of Romello stood and said, "Today's service is titled: God will help you right where you stand." Music was played, songs were sung, two young girls by the name of Kendyl and Kayla did a beautiful praise dance, and adult members even stood up to tell stories about how God helped them from the choices made in their youth. The youth group based the service on Isaiah 41:10," Fear not, for I am with you" are the words Crystal spoke as she continued with the scripture.

At the end of the service, the young lady whom Grannie had overheard came and said, "Hi, my name is Brenda; I was told you're the reason for the invite. I'm the reason it took so long for us to come. I'm the oldest at the youth center, and everyone looks up to me. When I said no each week, so did the others. But Ms. Joyce told me last weekend how you overheard us talking and came to the youth center. First, I thought you were crazy—with all due respect. But then I realized something my mom had said before she died. She said, "There's a time for everything." After hearing all the stories from people just like me today, I believe God will help me, and you inviting us here was right on time."

Grannie was thrilled. "Brenda, thanks for sharing those words. I'm far from crazy, and I'm just happy that you all made it today. God is always right on time."

You can read:
Ecclesiastes 3:1-8 and Isaiah 41:10 to learn more.

Who is Satan?

GRANNIE IS ENJOYING ANOTHER BEAUTIFUL day on the porch when she sees Wallace and Kirk walking along the sidewalk, bouncing a basketball. The ball bounces a little too high and lands in Grannie's yard. Kirk is the youngest at nine years old, and Wallace is 13.

Kirk ran to the gate and asked, "Excuse me, can we get our ball?"

Grannie answered, "Yes, you may, and thanks for asking. You don't hear many kids asking anymore. Where are you young men from?"

Kirk replied, "We just moved in down the street."

Just then Wallace screamed, "You little dummy! Mom said not to tell anyone our business! Why can't you listen, stupid?"

Grannie looked shocked and said, "Now, young man, what is your name?" Wallace looked at her but didn't say another word. What the young boys didn't know was that earlier that day, Grannie saw their mom and went over to say hi. The two ladies talked for a few hours, and their mom told Grannie all about the boys.

Grannie looked at Kirk and told the young man, "I believe you live close enough to run and ask your mom to come here, please. Can you do that?"

Kirk said, "Yes!" with excitement, grabbed the ball, and left Wallace there with Grannie.

"Wallace, you may sit on the porch and have yourself a glass of lemonade."

Wallace responded, "No thanks, I'm good."

"Young man, may I ask you a question?"

"Yes."

"Why do you use mean words to make a point? Meanness comes from Satan!"

Wallace said very angrily, "No I don't, and who is Satan?" He then sat on the steps and a puzzled look came over his face.

Grannie sighed. "I'll tell you who he is. He was a beautiful, knowledgeable, gifted angel who wanted to overpower God and take his throne. God didn't allow that to happen and put him out of Heaven, along with many other angels that took Satan's side. The moment he was put out of Heaven, all of God's light he once had, left him. He and the other angels became mean angels of darkness. Most people know them as demons. Everything he does is to hurt others. Satan is the ruler of mean words and actions. He loves when we speak words to discourage others and steal other people's joy. You did those same things when you called your little brother a dummy and stupid."

Wallace said rudely, "I say it all the time. He's okay."

Grannie said, "Okay, dummy, you're right."

Wallace stood up and said, "That wasn't nice. Why would you say that to me?"

Grannie just looked at him. Wallace looked at Grannie and said, "All right, I understand. I don't want to be mean like Satan."

"Most people don't" agreed Grannie. "The words and actions we pick show if we are doing good like God, or becoming mean like Satan. We need to speak words that will encourage a person when they do mess up. You can still tell them the truth without being mean. Satan is angry because he can never live in Heaven again and he knows we can—if we believe in Jesus and do our part to live by God's Commandments. Satan had it all; his name was Lucifer, which meant light bearer. He lost that name after being cast out of Heaven. Satan became his new name, which means adversary and enemy. You can be better, Wallace. It's not always easy to watch what you say. We have the choice to use better words, and over time, you learn to think before speaking."

Just then Kirk and his mom walked through the gate. Wallace told Kirk, "I don't think you're a dummy or stupid. I just want you to remember what Mom said." I have to look out for you little brother.

Kirk said, "I know I'm not. A dummy can't beat you in basketball."

You can read:
Ephesians 4:29, James 3:8-9 and Isaiah 14:12-14, Proverbs 15:1, Proverbs 18:21 and Psalm 34:13 to learn more.

How can I say thank you?

GRANNIE WAS INVITED TO A celebration luncheon and was asked to speak. People from the neighborhood nominated Grannie, but at first, she didn't want to attend. It took Grannie's children to talk her into attending, and the only reason Grannie said yes was to see her family home outside of their normal visiting schedule.

A lady stood up and said, "You have all spent many years helping others, no matter their age. We can always count on you and tonight; we celebrate you!"

Grannie stood up and replied, "Thank you all so much, and how lovely it is to be celebrated. I love food, and gifts are always nice." Everyone laughed. "Years ago, when I was a young girl, I got myself in some tough jams and didn't know what to do. But I'd remember what my mother would always say, Monk (that was my nickname) when life gets hard, or you make some wrong choices, always remember that God loves you no matter what you do. I can promise He's waiting for you to ask for help, and all you have to do is just believe."

"Those words were needed and heeded," said Grannie. "When I was in the worst jam of my life, I called on God, and He showed up. God saved me from all the jams I got myself into. Many have asked over the years, how did God show up and you never saw Him? I love that question, and the answer never changes. He showed up by using others to help me, to teach me, to listen to me, and most importantly, He showed up every time I read His word and asked for understanding. I've lived the best I can ever since." Grannie said, "I asked the Lord one day, how can I say thank you to you?

"A few days after I asked that very question, I saw an 80-year-old lady by the name of Gloria who needed some help. *No big deal*, I thought, *I can help.* Now, I need you to remember, I was young like you back in those days!" Everyone laughed, and Grannie went on speaking. "A few days after that, I saw some kids who needed help, and again I thought, no big deal, they needed help, and I was right there. Then a few days after that I met a gentleman who also needed help, and when he said thank you it made me feel a certain way; it was the way he said thank you. At that moment, I realized that helping others would be the way I would tell the Lord thank you for saving me. The Lord is still helping me help others; He places me in the right places at the right time. The man I helped over 40 years ago became my husband." Grannie smiled at the memory.

"I won't keep you much longer. The point I'm making is this; we should all show thankfulness to others, but most importantly, to the Lord. We can thank God and His Son, Jesus, by doing for others, with a smile; your time, prayers, food, laughter, gifts, and whatever your heart tells you. Ask God, how can I tell you, thank you? You may not notice at first glance, but I promise He will answer your question." Grannie paused a moment to let that sink in.

"I didn't want to come out today. I don't do anything for the praise of me. But my family made me realize that this was just another way of God showing Himself to me. Thank you all for celebrating us as we also celebrate you!"

You can read:
Ephesians 5:20, Galatians 5:22 and Psalm 106:1-2 to learn more.

How do I share Jesus with my friends?

§

MARLON, ONE OF THE NEIGHBORHOOD teens, is home for summer break. Grannie hasn't seen him since he went off to college in the fall. All the kids are happy about summer, and the neighborhood keeps busy this time of year. Marlon and Grannie have a seat on the porch, and as always, Grannie has cold lemonade.

"Well, Marlon, how was your first year of college?" asked Grannie. Marlon started to look sad. Grannie noticed and said, "Is it that bad?"

At that moment, Marlon started saying everything that had gone wrong during his first year in college. "It's hard to live for God and be in college, Grannie. Everything around me is the opposite of the word of God. There are parties every weekend, beautiful girls all around me, and some of my friends understand less about God than Jordan and I did."

Grannie nodded thoughtfully. "I see. Would you like some lemonade?" Grannie realized he needed to talk and clear his mind.

Marlon started talking about a group of three students who were made fun of on campus. "They get picked on all the time, yet they keep standing up for God."

Grannie asked, "Are these three your friends?"

Marlon replied with his head down, "No, ma'am. My friends are the ones I hang out with at the parties. They're good people, but I don't know how to share Jesus with them."

Grannie questioned him, "Why don't you hang out with the three you spoke of?"

Marlon shook his head. "I can't be treated that way. No one talks to them or wants to spend time with them."

Grannie didn't say a word; she just sipped her lemonade. Not saying many words was a little secret that Grannie learned from her Mema (grandmother). Sometimes a person just needs to hear themselves to see the answer is already there; all the listener has to do is ask the  right questions. It worked. Marlon looked at Grannie and said, "I know they're the ones I should be around, but my friends said they're too holy for fun. They even asked me to hang out with them one day, but I picked my friends instead—and had the worst day of my life. I'm still reading my Bible, and I know not everyone will be for me because I'm for Jesus. I just didn't think it would be this hard."

Grannie continued guiding him. "How can next year be better?"

Marlon thought a moment. "I'll make better choices this fall, and if my friends don't like my choices, I guess they were never real friends." Grannie smiled and raised her glass of lemonade to him.

Marlon laughed. "Grannie, have I ever told you I love you? You give the best advice." Marlon stood up and gave Grannie a hug and told her he would see her later. With a smile on her face, Grannie gathered the lemonade and cups from the table and headed inside.

Summer was coming to an end. June was in middle school now, involved in after-school activities, which gave Grannie some extra time. She had always wanted to play the piano, and now was as good a time to learn. Before leaving for her lessons one day, the phone rang.

Grannie: Hello?
Marlon: Hello, Grannie, this is Marlon.
Grannie: How is everything going? You sound good!
Marlon: Everything is going well. I made some changes on campus. I started going to Bible study with Shelly. It's cool, even fun some days. I lost a few friends once I stopped going to the parties. My friend Floyd started asking me why I was changing. I told him, "I'm not changing; I'm finally myself!" And now he comes to Bible study with us!

Grannie: I'm happy to hear about your friend. What about being picked on? That was one of the reasons you didn't hang out with the other three before.

Marlon: Yes, ma'am. Aaron and Jaron don't worry about what people say. Seeing them and how they keep moving forward has encouraged Floyd and me to do the same. I viewed them wrong; the three of them are cool to hang out with, and we learn many things together. We go everywhere together. I understand now you can live right *and* have fun. We're going to drive and see my parents and Jordan next weekend. May I bring everyone by to meet you?

Grannie: Now, you know you'd better not come to town and not see Grannie! I can't wait to see the awesome five together.

Marlon: Thanks for always listening. This year may be hard, but I'm only focused on the good.

They laughed together as they ended the call.

As Grannie reached for her car keys heading to piano lessons, she had a very special look on her face and said a prayer. "Lord, help these young people to live for you and understand that the best way to share Jesus is just by being themselves and letting your light shine through them. Amen."

You can read:
Matthew 5:13-16, 2 Timothy 3:12 to learn more.

What should I do if I mess up, God?

Grannie receives a very special call today, from a young man she met years ago when the church attended the local jail. The young man found his way to Grannie, and God used that moment to change his life.

    Grannie: Hello, Robert, what a nice surprise!
    Robert: How are you, Mrs. Givens?
    Grannie: I'm doing well, young man, and even better now to hear from you.

(Not everyone calls Grannie, Grannie. There are times her birth name is used. The day the church went to speak with inmates at the jail, Robert was told he would be talking with Mattie Givens, and they only had one hour.)

Robert: Mrs. Givens, I wanted to call and tell you what has happened in my life, and say thank you for the letters.

Grannie: You're welcome and yes, share this good news.

Robert: Well, you know I messed up, that's how I ended up in jail. I thought stealing money would allow me to be seen as this tough guy to my friends. I have learned so much since I got out of jail. But something was missing, and reading your last letter a few weeks ago helped me to understand what.

Grannie: All right, but I need you to remind me what stood out to you.

Robert: The part when you said no matter how many times I mess up in life, God will still be there, ready with open arms when I make that choice to come to him. The Lord will never leave or forsake me. You also stated that God would forgive me if I ask him, and will give me a fresh start. And I should ask those I hurt to forgive me; then I would see things clearly and know where to go from there.

(Robert got a little choked up and had to pause a moment.)

Robert (cont'd): Mrs. Givens, last week I went to the stores and the homes of the places I took money from, and I asked them to forgive me. Some people did, and a few did not, but I was able to look at them and own up to what I did. I was even able to give a few of them back what I took. I felt free! I know I still have some ways to go, but now I understand I can be forgiven. I'm moving forward, and I just wanted you to know, I understand.

Grannie: Robert, you keep thinking like that and making the right choices, even when it's hard, you will always be all right. You have a story to tell that will help others. Robert, what you did took courage, and thank you for sharing that with me. People don't realize it; stories like yours remind me that so many people could have a better life and understanding of the truth when someone takes the time to help them see clearly.

The two ended their phone call, and Grannie was in tears, but she wasn't sad, she was happy and thankful for Robert. She looked up and said, "God, thank you for always showing your greatness."

You can read:
Ephesians 4:28 and 1 John 1:9,
Matthew 6:15 and Matthew 18:21-22 to learn more.

What does it mean the Bible is alive?

A FEW WEEKS BEFORE JUNE started middle school; she asked Grannie a question that would make Grannie speechless for the first time. It wasn't that Grannie didn't understand the question, and it wasn't that Grannie didn't know for herself, but Grannie didn't know the right way to explain it to June.

June asked Grannie, "how is the Bible alive?"

Grannie paused for a moment in thought, then said, "June, next time you come over I'll have an answer for you." Grannie spent the week reading and praying for the right way to answer this question. She knew that June listened to her, and Grannie understood this question had to be answered just right.

Sunday came, and as Grannie listened to the singers in church, her mind was still on June's question. Just then Pastors Johnson and Page spoke on the topic: The Bible lives in you, and the Bible is alive. "The book of Hebrews tells us it's powerful!" said Pastor Page, who spoke on the power that comes from knowing and understanding what the Bible tells us. Pastor Johnson spoke on how the word of God becomes a part of you. Like the heartbeat we need daily to live, we need God's word daily to live. Just then Grannie knew how she would answer June's question.

Instead of waiting for June to come over, Grannie called and asked June's parents if she could pick her up for ice cream later that day. June's mom said, "I would like some ice cream too, Mom!"

Grannie laughed and said, "I'll be there to pick you both up later today." Grannie arrived, and June ran out the door. Oh, how she loved to see Grannie! But she was even more excited that here mom was coming along. June's dad was Grannie's youngest son, but Grannie loved June's mom just as much.

Grannie told June's mom everything that took place and why she had to speak with June that day after thinking about this question all week. The three of them had a great time at the ice cream shop, and then Grannie said, "June, the Bible is alive because God is real and he inspired the words in that unique book. It was written by everyday people, such as you, me, and your mom. God's power is inside the pages, and so is his truth and knowledge. The Bible is how he chose to teach us and share with us the correct way to live day by day."

June's mom said, "I never thought of it that way." Then she asked June, "Do you understand?"

June said, "Yes, Mommy, the Bible is alive because God is real, full of power, and God loves us enough to make His words come true."

Grannie looked at June in amazement and said, "How is it that I answered you, but you just taught me the meaning?" They all laughed and enjoyed the rest of their ice cream.

You can read:
Hebrews 4:12 to learn more.

God, do you like to laugh?

§

GRANNIE IS ON A PHONE call with her grandson, Tyler.

Tyler: Grannie, do you remember when you read we are all made in God's image?
Grannie: Yes.
Tyler: I wanted to know if God has time to laugh. I love to laugh and make others laugh. In fact, I should be in comedy!

(Grannie laughed just from listening to the way he said his last statement.)

Grannie: Yes, God does laugh. When people think they can mock God, he laughs. I also believe God loves to laugh. Have you seen the beautiful but funny flowers, animals, and fish? I'm going to grab my book that has all types of creatures God made. You get your computer ready so you can pull up the pictures, and we can view the pictures together.

Komondor Dog- Long haired mop dog.

Angora rabbit- Furry long eared domestic rabbit.

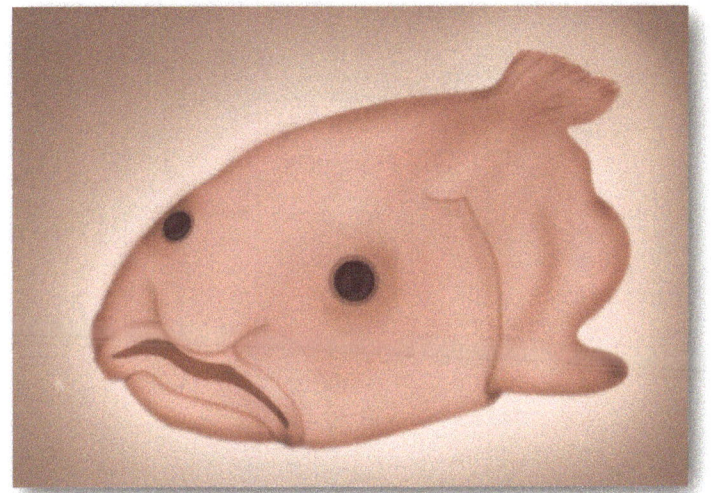

Blob fish- Sea fish from the deep coast waters.

A young box fish- Related to the pufferfish.

Hooker's Lips – A flower that always blow a kiss.

Bee Orchid- A flower that looks like a bird or bee.

(Tyler laughed very hard.)

Tyler: Grannie, this is neat! I believe God does like to laugh. He has made some amazing and funny creatures. I also noticed he likes color and design; everything has its own identity.

Grannie: Grandson, these are just a handful of amazing creations. We are surrounded by natural beauty of the Creator, all we have to do is open our eyes and see. You keep making people laugh, grandson. Laughter has a beauty of its own.

You can read:
Genesis 1:25-29 and Psalm 2:4 to learn more.

I hope you enjoyed these stories, if after reading you have decided you would like to open your heart to God, all you have to say is "Jesus is Lord and believe in your heart that God raised him from the dead, you will be saved. For with the heart one believes and is justified, and with the mouth, one confesses and is saved." (New King James, Rom. 10.9-11).

All we have to do is say sorry which means repent for all you have done wrong, and do your best to live better from this point on. God will help you live better through his son, Jesus and his Holy Spirit.

If you have questions or need someone to talk to, feel free to reach out to Grannie at: grannieknowsbeststories@gmail.com or Like Grannie on Facebook: https://www.facebook.com/Grannie-Knows-Best-Bedtime-Stories-324070177930781/
Until next time,
Grannie

"New King James Version (NKJV Bible)". The Bible Gateway. Retrieved 2011-09-14. Peterson, The Holy Bible, New King James Version. Nashville: Nelson. 1982.

www.ingramcontent.com/pod-product-compliance
Lightning Source LLC
Chambersburg PA
CBHW061936290426
44113CB00025B/2935